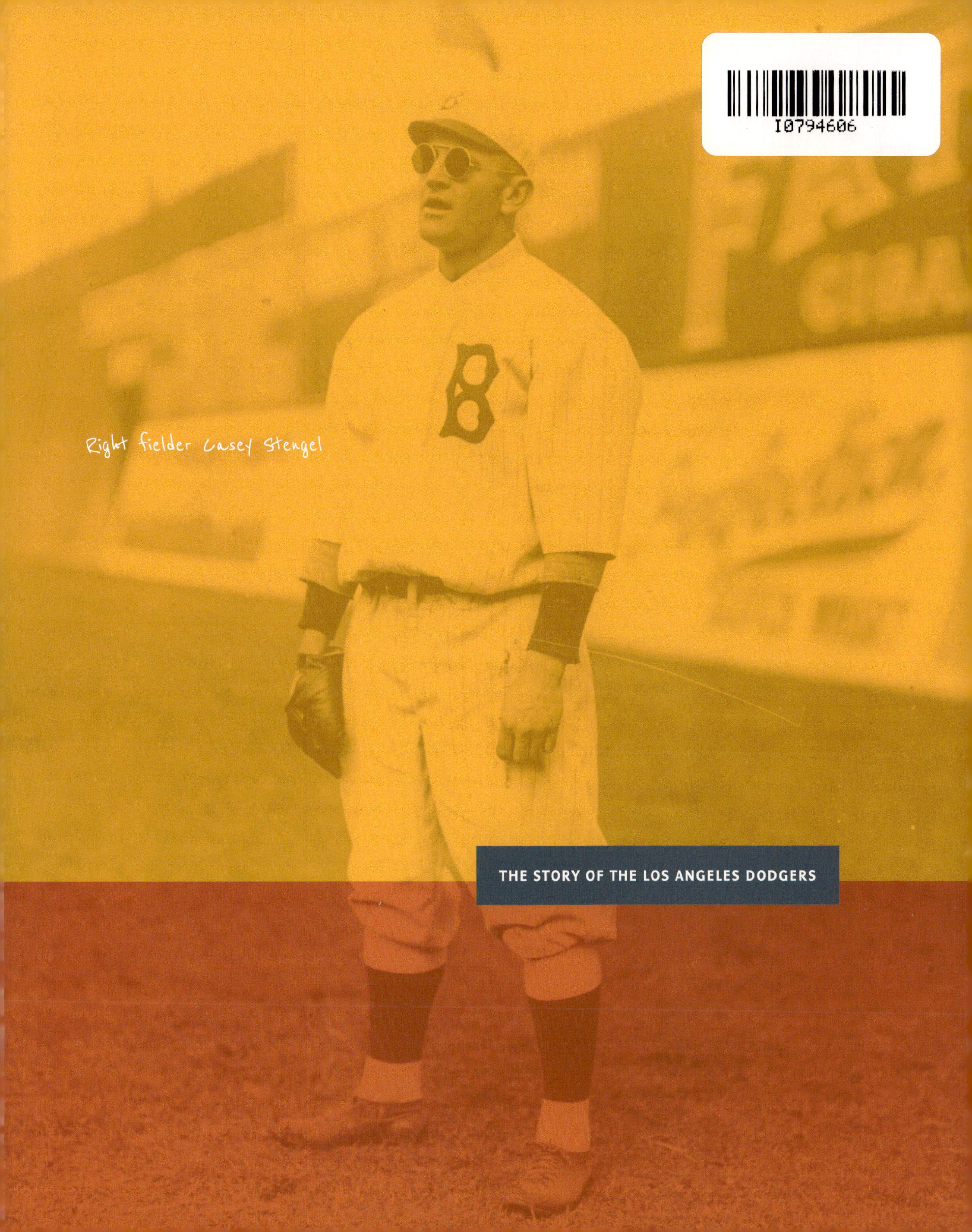

Right fielder Casey Stengel

THE STORY OF THE LOS ANGELES DODGERS

First baseman Freddie Freeman

THE STORY OF THE

LOS ANGELES DODGERS

JIM WHITING

CREATIVE SPORTS

Pitcher Sandy Koufax

CREATIVE EDUCATION / CREATIVE PAPERBACKS

Published by Creative Education and Creative Paperbacks
P.O. Box 227, Mankato, Minnesota 56002
Creative Education and Creative Paperbacks are imprints of
The Creative Company
www.thecreativecompany.us

Book Design by Wyeth Morgan
Art direction by Blue Design (www.bluedes.com)

Images by Alamy Stock Photo/Cal Sport Media, 26-27; Associated Press/Ashley Landis, cover, Doug Pizac, 22-23, Marcio Jose Sanchez, 6 (bottom, left); Getty Images/B Bennett, 9, Bettmann, 10, 15, Bob Gomel, 3, Daniel Shirey, 2, Diamond Images, 18, Ed Jackson/New York Daily News Archive, 16, Focus On Sport, 7 (bottom, right), Jeff Gross, 6 (bottom, right), John Dominis/Time Life Pictures, 10, 11, Justin Sullivan, 7 (top, left), Katelyn Mulcahy, 30, Louis Requena, 25, Mary Decicco, 31, Photo File, cover, 6 (top, right), 7 (bottom, left), 19, Robert Riger, 4-5, 32, Scott Halleran, 20, Will Hart, 29, William Vandivert/Time Life Pictures, 6 (top, left); Library of Congress/public domain, 1; Public Domain/Detroit Public Library, 7 (top, right); Wikimedia Commons/George Dorrill, 12

Library of Congress Cataloging-in-Publication Data
Names: Whiting, Jim, 1943- author
Title: The story of the Los Angeles Dodgers / by Jim Whiting.
Description: Mankato, Minnesota : Creative Education and Creative Paperbacks, [2026] | Series: Creative sports. Major League baseball | Includes index. | Audience: Ages 8-12 | Audience: Grades 4-6 | Summary: "Discover the Los Angeles Dodgers' thrilling journey from Brooklyn roots to modern triumphs, featuring legendary players, historic victories, and the Major League Baseball team's unforgettable moments. Written for middle-grade readers. Includes table of contents, sidebars, and index"– Provided by publisher.
Identifiers: LCCN 2025013112 (print) | LCCN 2025013113 (ebook) | ISBN 9798895810972 library binding | ISBN 9798896800507 paperback | ISBN 9798895812235 ebook
Subjects: LCSH: Los Angeles Dodgers (Baseball team)–History–Juvenile literature | Baseball–California–History–20th century–Juvenile literature
Classification: LCC GV875.L6 W425 2026 (print) | LCC GV875.L6 (ebook)
LC record available at https://lccn.loc.gov/2025013112
LC ebook record available at https://lccn.loc.gov/20.

Printed in the United States

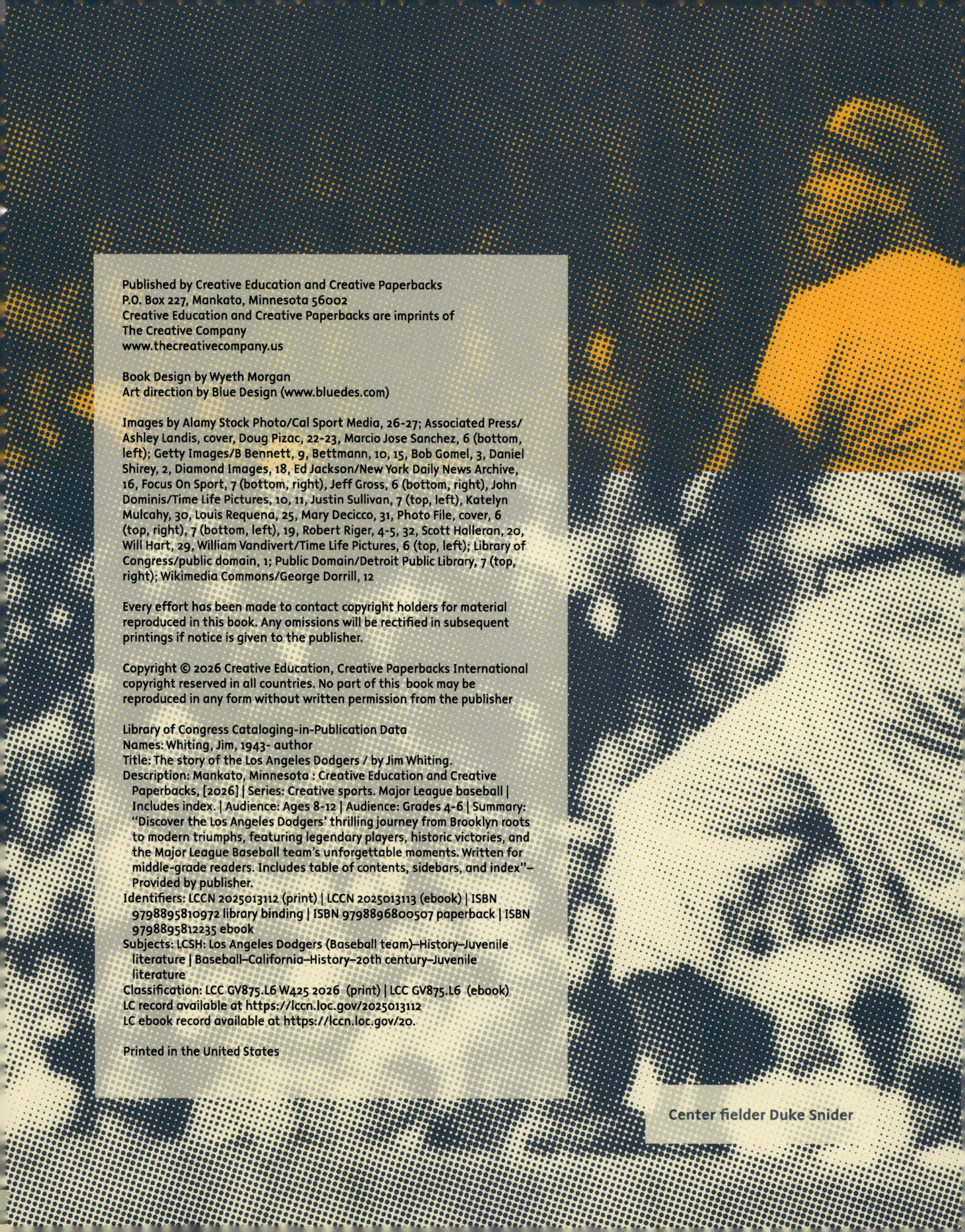

Center fielder Duke Snider

EP 27
Dodgers
Dodgers
Dodgers
Dodgers

LA
Dodgers

LA
Dodgers

LONEY
7

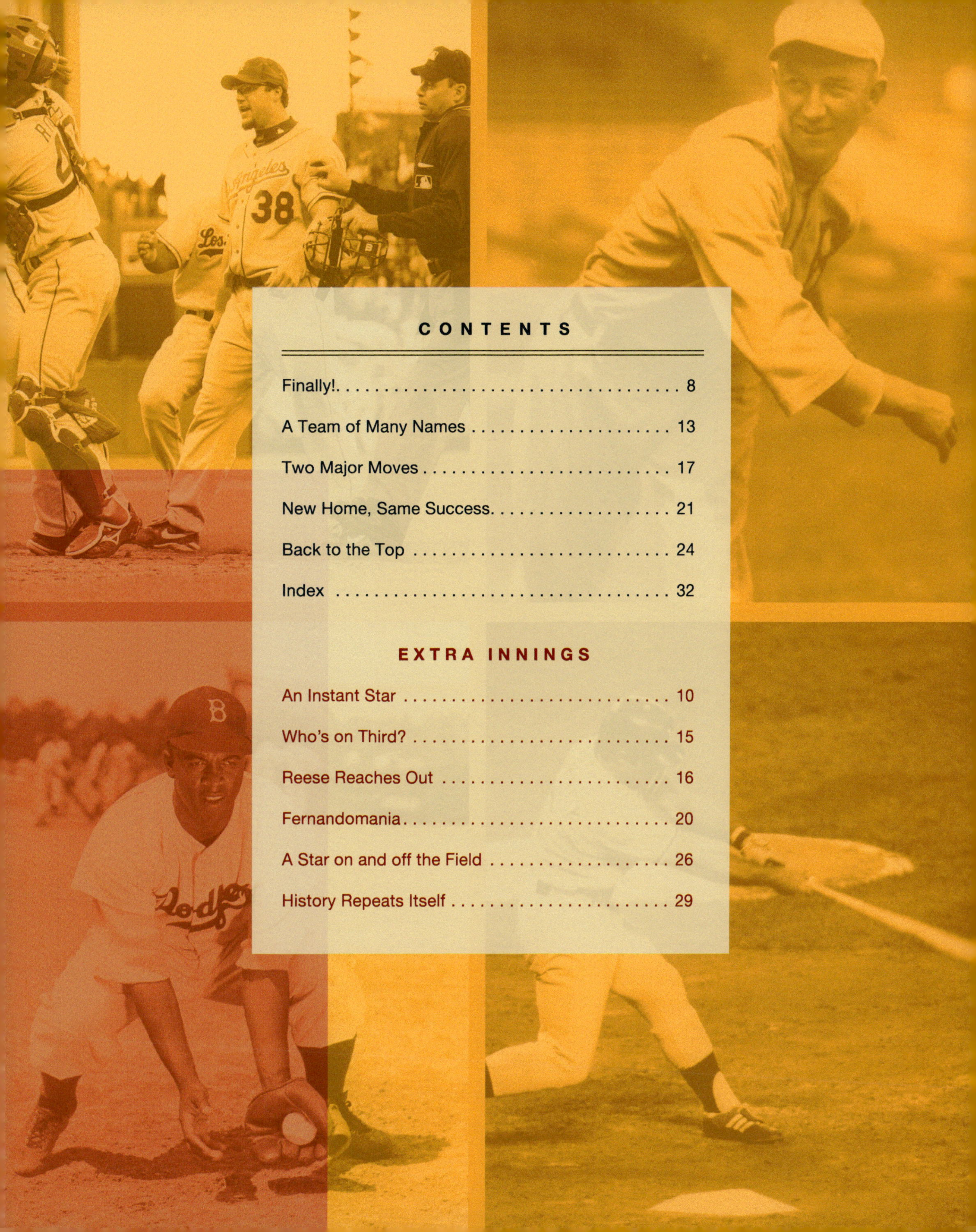

CONTENTS

EXTRA INNINGS

FINALLY!

The 1955 World Series matched the New York Yankees and Brooklyn Dodgers. The Yankees were favored. They had already won 16 times in the series' 52-year history. Brooklyn had appeared in the "Fall Classic" seven times. They had never won. The last five defeats had been to the Yankees, most recently in 1952 and 1953.

The teams split the first six games. Dodgers manager Walter Alston chose Johnny Podres to pitch the decisive Game 7. Podres had been the winning pitcher in Game 3. But he was only 22 and in just his third season. Despite his youth, Podres was supremely confident. On the bus to the game, Podres shouted, "Get me one today, just get me one run."

The game was scoreless in the bottom of the third. Podres gave up a walk and a single with two outs. The next batter hit a ground ball toward third base. The ball struck Yankee shortstop Phil Rizzuto, who was sliding into the base and couldn't avoid it. Under baseball rules, he was out. "In all those Series, there was always some strange play that the Yankees made and we didn't that turned the last game," said Dodgers pitcher Carl Erskine. "Seeing

Pitcher Johnny Podres

EXTRA INNINGS

ROY CAMPANELLA
CATCHER
DODGERS SEASONS: 1948–57
HEIGHT: 5-FOOT-9
WEIGHT: 190 POUNDS
KEY STATS: .276 BATTING AVERAGE, 242 HOME RUNS, 856 RBIS, 8X ALL-STAR

AN INSTANT STAR

In 1948, Roy Campanella became the first Black catcher in Major League Baseball (MLB) after spending nearly a decade in the Negro Leagues. He quickly made up for lost time. He took over as the team's regular catcher midway through his first season. In 1949, he joined Jackie Robinson and Don Newcombe as the first Black All-Stars. Two years later, "Campy" hit 33 home runs and drove in 108 runs with a .325 batting average. He was named National League Most Valuable Player (MVP). He repeated that honor in 1953 and 1955. Tragically, a car crash in 1958 paralyzed him and ended his playing career. Baseball expert Bill James named Campanella the third-best catcher of all time. In 1969, he became just the second Black player elected to the Baseball Hall of Fame.

First baseman Gil Hodges

Rizzuto called out to end that inning, I thought, that's an omen. Things like that usually happened to us."

Podres got his run in the fourth inning. Catcher Roy Campanella doubled to deep left field. First baseman Gil Hodges hit a sharp single to left field that scored Campanella.

Podres got another run in the sixth inning. Hodges came up with the bases loaded. He hit a sacrifice fly to center/right field that plated shortstop Pee Wee Reese.

The Yankees threatened to score in the bottom of that inning on a walk and a single with no outs. Catcher Yogi Berra lofted a long fly ball into the left field corner. The runner on first, Gil McDougald, was sure that the ball would fall in for an extra-base hit. He rounded second base. But left fielder Sandy Amoros sprinted after the ball and made one of the greatest catches in World Series history. He slammed on the brakes and threw the ball to Reese. Reese threw to Hodges, who tagged out McDougald trying to scramble back to first base after realizing that Amoros had caught the ball.

Podres faced one more challenge. Two singles in the eighth put runners on first and third with one out. A short fly ball into right field wasn't deep enough for the runner on third to tag up and score. Podres struck out the next batter.

Morisco

The score was still 2–0 in the bottom of the ninth. Podres got the first batter to ground out. The next one flew out to left field. Reese threw out the third batter.

"When Pee Wee threw out Elston Howard for the final out, we swamped Podres at the mound," Erskine said. "But on the way up the ramp to our clubhouse, after finally winning the World Series, we were more reverential than boisterous. Before the writers came in, there was no noise."

The long wait was over. The Brooklyn Dodgers were World Series champions!

A TEAM OF MANY NAMES

The Los Angeles Dodgers boast one of the most distinguished histories in Major League Baseball (MLB). The team began playing in Brooklyn, a borough of New York City. The team was called the Brooklyn Atlantics. It became part of the American Association in 1884. The following year, the team changed its name to Brooklyn Grays. Three years later, it became the Bridegrooms. The team joined the National League (NL) in 1890. Outfielder Oyster Burns had a league-leading 128 runs batted in (RBIs) that year. The Bridegrooms won the pennant.

In 1899, the franchise became the Superbas. The team topped the NL in 1899 and 1900. It featured right fielder Willie Keeler. Just 5-foot-4, he was nicknamed "Wee Willie." Keeler was known for a simple strategy: "Hit 'em where they ain't." The franchise became the Dodgers in 1911. A multitude of trolley cars zipped through Brooklyn streets in those days. Fans coming to

Right fielder Willie Keeler

games were called "trolley dodgers." They had to be careful to avoid being hit by the cars.

In 1914, the team became the Robins. The name honored its popular manager, Wilbert Robinson. The Robins reached the World Series in 1916 and 1920. They lost both times. The team added a few good players in the 1920s. One was pitcher Dazzy Vance. He led the NL in strikeouts from 1922 to 1928. Another was outfielder Babe Herman. He hit .339 in seven seasons. But his fielding was inconsistent. "Every fly ball was an adventure for Babe," said catcher Al López.

Robinson retired in 1931. The team name returned to Dodgers. During the 1930s, fans referred to the team as the "Daffy Dodgers." Many players were more famous for their faults than their talents. Still, Brooklyn fans loved the bungling team. They lovingly referred to the Dodgers as "Dem Bums."

Toward the end of the 1930s, fiery manager Leo Durocher took over. The Dodgers quickly improved. The roster featured talented players such as shortstop Pee Wee Reese and first baseman Dolph Camilli. The Dodgers stormed to the 1941 NL pennant. They met the mighty Yankees in the World Series. The Yankees took a two-games-to-one lead. The Dodgers won Game 3. They led 4–3 in the ninth inning of Game 4. A win would tie the series. There were two outs and two strikes on the batter. He swung and missed. But catcher Mickey Owen missed the ball, too. The batter ran to first base. That changed the course of the game. The Yankees scored four runs and won. The next day, New York captured the series.

BABE HERMAN
OUTFIELDER

WHO'S ON THIRD?

BOSTON BRAVES AT BROOKLYN DODGERS

AUGUST 10, 1926

With one out and the bases loaded, Dodgers rookie outfielder Babe Herman hit a long fly ball to right field. It caromed off the wall. The runner on third scored easily. Pitcher Dazzy Vance had been on second. He rounded third but turned around and went back to the bag. Second baseman Chick Fewster had been on second. He saw Vance head for home. He didn't see him turn around. He raced to third. In the meantime, Herman had motored into second. When he saw that the Boston right fielder had thrown home, he continued on to third. Now there were three Dodgers standing on third base! The Boston third baseman tagged all three of them. He even tagged the umpire, who ruled that Fewster and Vance were both out. Herman went on to have a sterling 13-year MLB career. He batted .324 with five teams and drove in nearly 1,000 runs. Yet he is primarily remembered for this bizarre play.

EXTRA INNINGS

Pee Wee Reese and Jackie Robinson

HAROLD "PEE WEE" REESE
SHORTSTOP
DODGERS SEASONS: 1940–42, 1946–58
HEIGHT: 5-FOOT-10
WEIGHT: 160 POUNDS
KEY STATS: .269 BATTING AVERAGE, 126 HOME RUNS, 885 RBIS, 10X ALL-STAR

REESE REACHES OUT

Before Jackie Robinson joined the Dodgers, several of the team's players drew up a petition. They did not want to play with him. They demanded to be traded. Even though he grew up in the South, Reese refused to sign the petition. He was one of the team's most respected members. The petition soon died. Early in the season, the Dodgers were warming up before a game in Cincinnati. Reds players and fans screamed obscenities at Robinson. Reese walked across the field. He put his hand on Robinson's shoulder. "He didn't say a word, but he looked over at the chaps who were yelling at me and just stared," Robinson said. The heckling stopped. In 2005, a statue was built at a Brooklyn ballfield to commemorate the moment.

TWO MAJOR MOVES

For many years, no MLB team would sign Black players. In the 1940s, Dodgers president Branch Rickey decided to end that practice. He made plans to integrate his team. The Dodgers scouted Negro League teams for the right man.

The "right man" was Jackie Robinson. Rickey signed him in late 1945. Robinson was a tremendous athlete. He was also a fierce competitor. Rickey could see Robinson's inner strength. He felt Robinson had "enough guts not to fight back" when racists confronted him. He was promoted to the Dodgers to begin the 1947 season. "They said the most hateful things in the world to Jackie," said right fielder Carl Furillo, "and it bothered him something fierce, but they only hurt themselves, as it just made Jackie play that much harder."

Robinson hit .297. He stole a league-leading 29 bases and scored 125 runs. The Dodgers won the pennant. Robinson earned MLB's first-ever Rookie of the Year award. He played nine more stellar seasons with the Dodgers. He became the first Black player in the Baseball Hall of Fame. Every MLB team has since retired his jersey number (42).

In 1949, the Dodgers won their third pennant of the decade. They also suffered their third World Series defeat. All three losses were to the Yankees. "Wait until next year!" became fans' unofficial rallying cry.

As the 1950s began, Brooklyn boasted a powerful lineup. The "Boys of Summer" included Robinson, catcher Roy Campanella, center fielder Duke Snider, and first baseman Gil Hodges. Pitchers Don Newcombe and Carl Erskine worked the mound.

In 1955, "next year" finally came. "It's like I died and went to heaven," said third baseman Jim Gilliam of the Dodgers' first World Series win. "I'm so happy we could finally do this for our fans."

Brooklyn won the NL pennant again the next season. Newcombe became the first pitcher to win both the Cy Young and Most Valuable Player (MVP) awards. Yet again, the Dodgers met the Yankees in the World Series. This time, the Yankees took the series in seven games.

A decade after breaking the color barrier, the Dodgers made the news again. The team moved to Los Angeles after the 1957 season. Its new home was Los Angeles Memorial Coliseum. It was used primarily for football. So the baseball field dimensions were unusual. Players could hit 250- foot home runs to left field over a 40-foot wall. Drives nearly 200 feet longer to right field were simply long outs.

The Dodgers captured the 1959 NL pennant. They faced the Chicago White Sox in the World Series. Los Angeles defeated the White Sox in six games. "I think our win in 1959 cemented the bond between the Los Angeles fans and the team," manager Walter Alston said. "That championship finally made us their team."

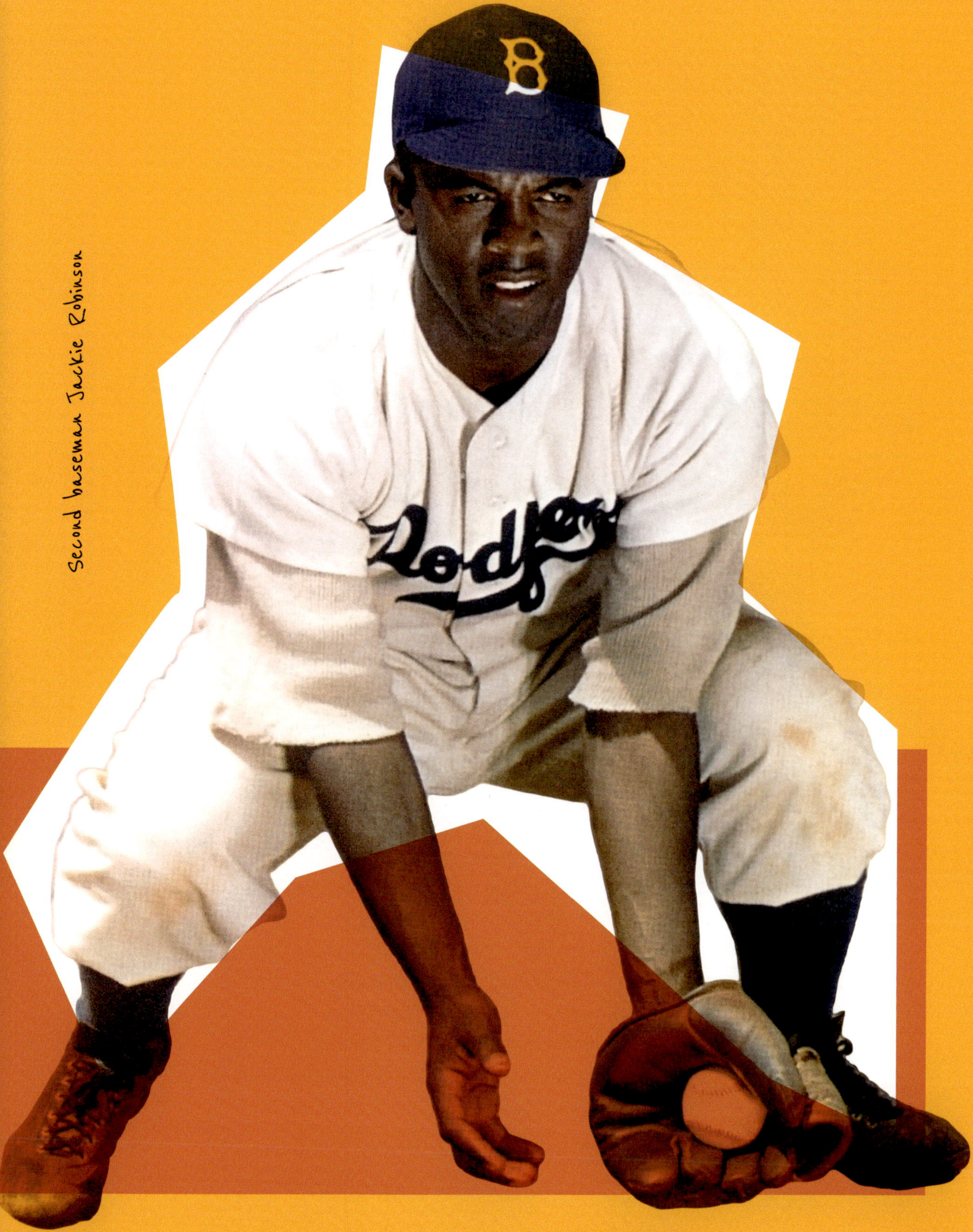

Second baseman Jackie Robinson

EXTRA INNINGS

FERNANDO VALENZUELA
PITCHER
DODGERS SEASONS: 1980–90
HEIGHT: 5-FOOT-11
WEIGHT: 180 POUNDS
KEY STATS: 141–116 WIN-LOSS RECORD, 3.31 ERA, 1759 STRIKEOUTS, 6X ALL-STAR

FERNANDOMANIA

Fernando Valenzuela created a sensation in 1981 when he was just 20 years old. He pitched a shutout in his first game. He won his next seven games as well. Four of those were shutouts. With that, "Fernandomania" was born. Valenzuela led MLB with 180 strikeouts. He won the Cy Young Award. He was also named Rookie of the Year. He was the first player to receive both honors in the same year. He pitched to sold-out stadiums. "I truly believe that there is no other player in major-league history who created more new fans than Fernando Valenzuela," said Dodgers broadcaster Jaime Jarrín. "Fernando turned so many people from Mexico, Central America, South America into fans."

NEW HOME, SAME SUCCESS

The Dodgers moved to the newly built Dodger Stadium in 1962. Following a tie in the regular season standings, the San Francisco Giants won a best-of-three series to decide the pennant. By then, the Dodgers' roster had been rebuilt. It featured lefty Sandy Koufax and righty Don Drysdale. They were two of the best pitchers in MLB. Maury Wills was a speedy, base-stealing shortstop. Hard-hitting outfielders Tommy Davis and Willie Davis led the offense.

In 1963, Los Angeles captured yet another pennant. The Dodgers faced their old rivals, the Yankees. This time, Los Angeles swept New York in four games. The Dodgers' pitchers allowed only four runs throughout the series. Two years later, the Dodgers topped the NL again. They faced the Minnesota Twins in the World Series. Koufax was in top form. He hurled a three-hit, complete-game shutout in Game 7.

Los Angeles shot back to the World Series in 1966. But the Baltimore Orioles swept the Dodgers in four games. In the following years, the team remained strong. Alston continued to provide steady leadership. He retired in 1976. Third base coach Tommy Lasorda replaced him. Lasorda was the opposite of the quiet, soft-spoken Alston in temperament. But he achieved the same results. The Dodgers remained an NL powerhouse.

Los Angeles reached the World Series in 1977 and 1978. They fell to the Yankees both times. In 1981, the two teams returned to the World Series yet again. This time, the Dodgers had a new weapon. Twenty-year-old rookie pitcher Fernando Valenzuela had burst onto the scene. Los Angeles was deep into "Fernandomania." Hysteria surrounded the team's young star. The Dodgers dropped the first two games. They won Game 3 behind Valenzuela's

Catcher Mike Piazza

strong arm. That inspired the team. It won the next three games and the series. "We had them on the ropes," said Yankees outfielder Dave Winfield, "but that kid [Valenzuela] turned the series around."

After that, the Dodgers had several disappointing seasons. They surprised fans in 1988 when they defeated the Oakland Athletics in the World Series. Oakland had the best record in MLB that season. It was the Dodgers' sixth championship. A major factor was pitcher Orel Hershiser. He set an MLB record with 59 consecutive scoreless innings during the regular season. Hershiser led the league with 23 wins, which included eight shutouts. He was a shoo-in for the Cy Young Award.

The 1990s were the first decade since the 1930s that the Dodgers did not appear in the World Series, even though they boasted winning records nearly every season. "We kept looking for the quick fix, and there is no such thing," said catcher Paul Lo Duca.

The Dodgers missed the playoffs between 1997 and 2003. In 2004, Los Angeles finally returned to the postseason. They fell to the St. Louis Cardinals in the National League Division Series (NLDS). They made the playoffs again two years later. The New York Mets swept them in three straight games in the NLDS. But better times lay ahead.

BACK TO THE TOP

By 2008, young stars had begun to emerge. Outfielder Matt Kemp, catcher Russell Martin, and pitcher Chad Billingsley moved up from the Dodgers' minor league system. Outfielder Manny Ramírez came from the Boston Red Sox. The result was an NL West title. The Dodgers swept

Third baseman Ron Cey

LA
10

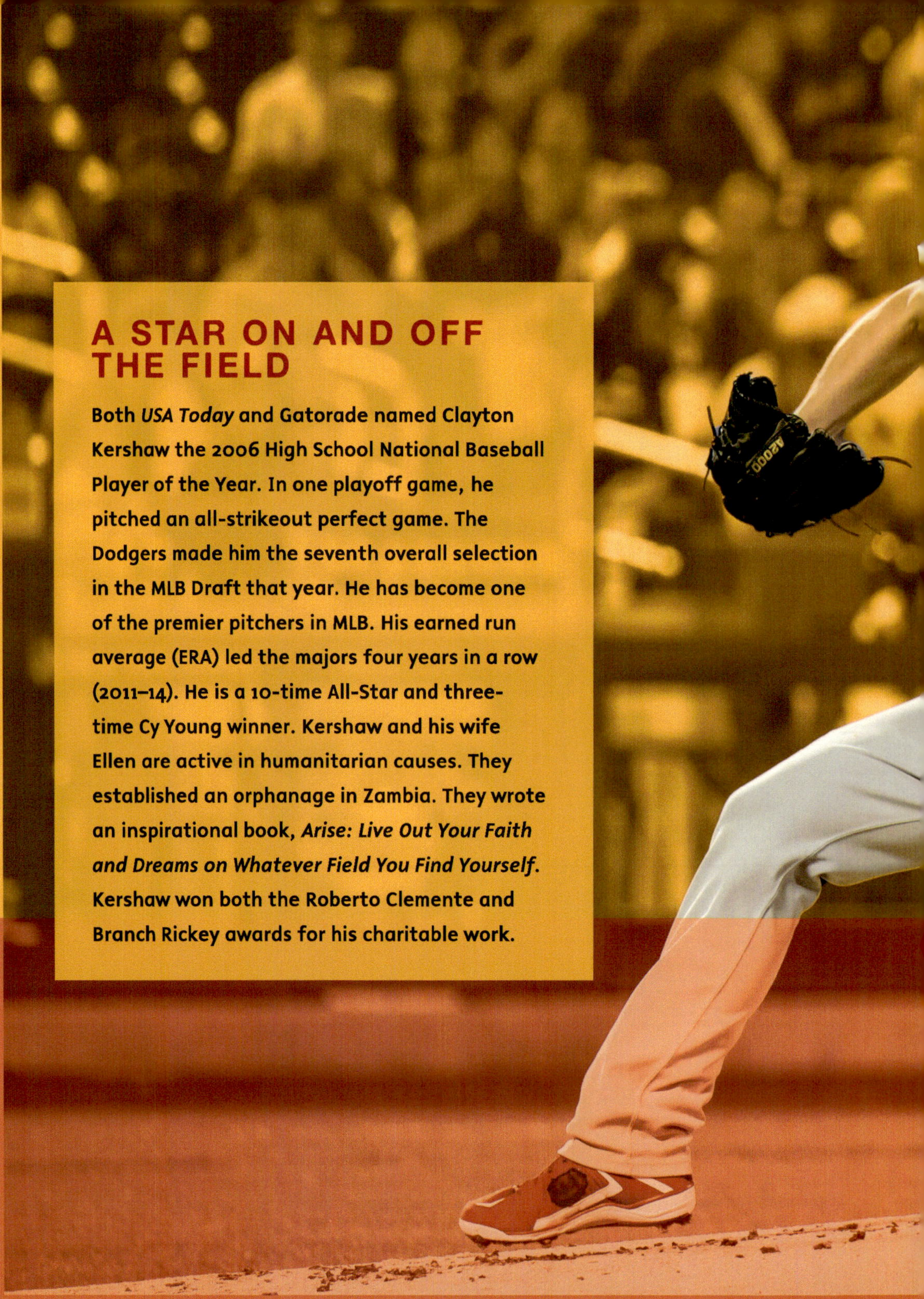

A STAR ON AND OFF THE FIELD

Both *USA Today* and Gatorade named Clayton Kershaw the 2006 High School National Baseball Player of the Year. In one playoff game, he pitched an all-strikeout perfect game. The Dodgers made him the seventh overall selection in the MLB Draft that year. He has become one of the premier pitchers in MLB. His earned run average (ERA) led the majors four years in a row (2011–14). He is a 10-time All-Star and three-time Cy Young winner. Kershaw and his wife Ellen are active in humanitarian causes. They established an orphanage in Zambia. They wrote an inspirational book, *Arise: Live Out Your Faith and Dreams on Whatever Field You Find Yourself*. Kershaw won both the Roberto Clemente and Branch Rickey awards for his charitable work.

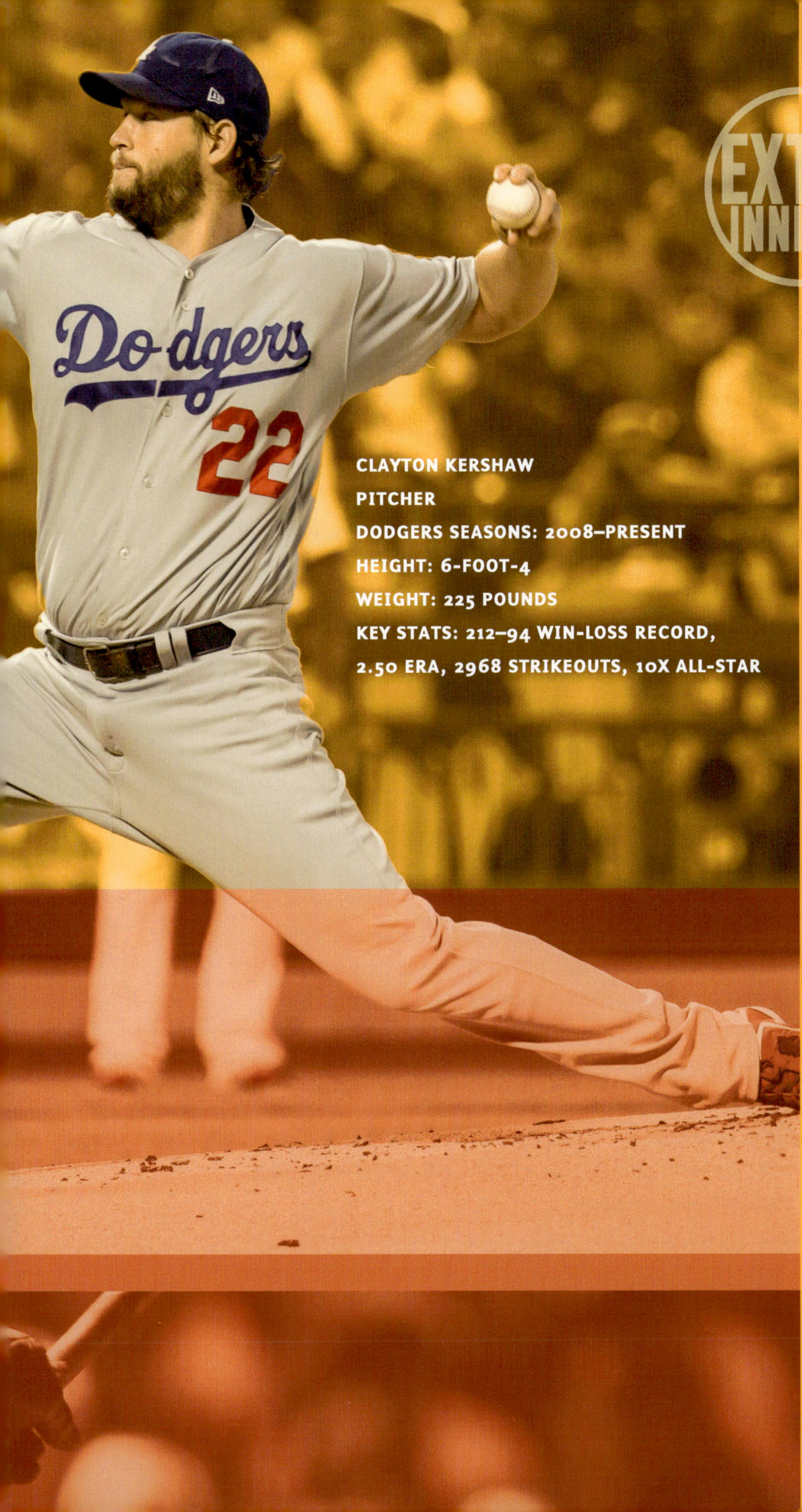

EXTRA INNINGS

CLAYTON KERSHAW

PITCHER

DODGERS SEASONS: 2008–PRESENT

HEIGHT: 6-FOOT-4

WEIGHT: 225 POUNDS

KEY STATS: 212–94 WIN-LOSS RECORD, 2.50 ERA, 2968 STRIKEOUTS, 10X ALL-STAR

the Chicago Cubs in the NLDS. But the Philadelphia Phillies knocked them out in the National League Championship Series (NLCS).

The Dodgers won the division title again in 2009. The Phillies stymied them again in the NLCS. After that, the Dodgers missed the playoffs for three years. One highlight was hard-throwing pitcher Clayton Kershaw. He won three Cy Young Awards in four years. He was also the league MVP in 2014.

In 2017, Los Angeles won 104 games. The Dodgers advanced to the World Series for the first time since 1988. But the Houston Astros defeated them, four games to three.

Los Angeles faced the Red Sox in the 2018 World Series. The Dodgers lost the first two games. Game 3 stretched to a World Series-record 18 innings. Los Angeles finally won. But that was their only win.

The Dodgers ran away with their seventh straight division title in 2019. They faced the Washington Nationals in the NLDS. The teams split the first four games. Los Angeles took an early 3–0 lead in the deciding Game 5. Washington tied the score late in the game. It won the game on a 10th-inning grand slam.

Los Angeles bounced back with a record of 43–17 in the 2020 season, which was shortened due to the COVID-19 pandemic. It was the best mark in MLB. The Dodgers swept through an eight-team NL tournament to determine the World Series participants. They won their seventh World Series title, four games to two over the Tampa Bay Rays. "This team was incredible all throughout the year, all throughout the postseason, all throughout the quarantine," said shortstop Corey Seager. "We never stopped."

The Dodgers continued their domination of the NL with a 106–56 record in 2022, an all-time franchise best 111 wins in 2022, and a 100–62 record in 2023. But they fell short of the World Series each time.

It was a different story in 2024. The Dodgers signed superstar Shohei Ohtani to a $700 million contract. It was the largest contract in MLB history at

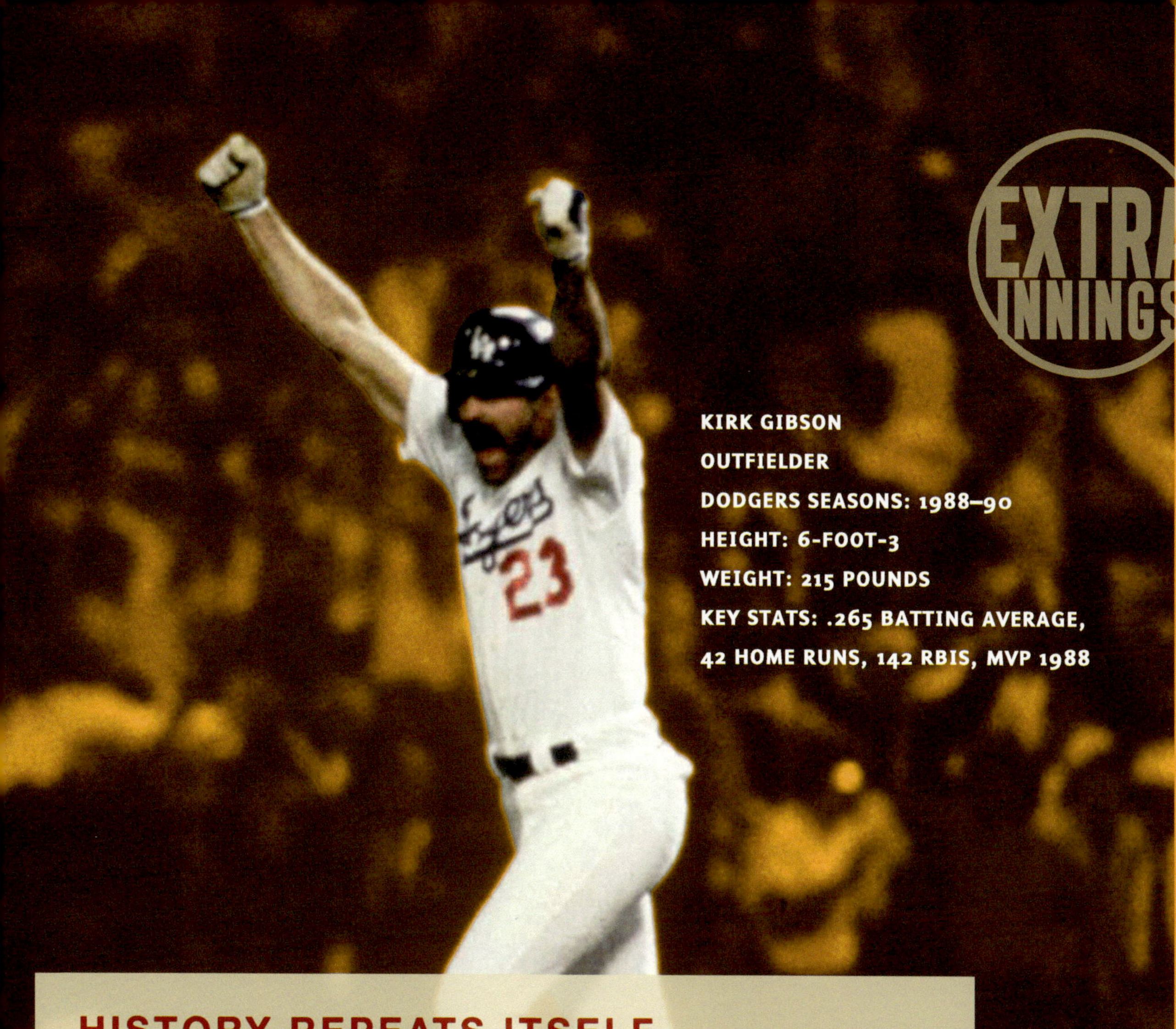

EXTRA INNINGS

KIRK GIBSON
OUTFIELDER
DODGERS SEASONS: 1988–90
HEIGHT: 6-FOOT-3
WEIGHT: 215 POUNDS
KEY STATS: .265 BATTING AVERAGE, 42 HOME RUNS, 142 RBIS, MVP 1988

HISTORY REPEATS ITSELF

In Game 1 of the 1988 World Series, the Dodgers trailed the Oakland Athletics 4–3 in the bottom of the ninth inning. With a runner on first and two outs, Kirk Gibson limped to the plate as a pinchhitter. Both legs were injured, and he could barely walk. Yet he smacked one of the most famous home runs in MLB history. The 5–4 win fueled the Dodgers. The team took the World Series title in five games. Thirty-six years later, Gibson was watching Game 1 of the World Series on television. It was the bottom of the 10th inning. Los Angeles trailed the Yankees 3–2. The Dodgers loaded the bases with two outs. First baseman Freddie Freeman came to the plate. Like Gibson, Freeman was injured, with a badly sprained ankle. "I felt the premonition that it was going to happen," Gibson said. "It was crazy." "Crazy" became reality as Freeman smashed the ball into the right field bleachers. "Freddie Freeman channeling his inner Kirk Gibson!" shouted the TV announcer. It was the first walkoff grand slam home run in World Series history. Los Angeles went on to win the Series in five games.

LA
Dodgers
17
new balance

Pitcher Blake Snell

that time. He became the first player with 50 home runs and 50 stolen bases. He was named the league's MVP. Coupled with two MVPs with the Los Angeles Angels, only Barry Bonds with seven has more. The Dodgers faced the Yankees in the World Series. Riding the momentum of a game-winning grand slam home run by first baseman Freddie Freeman in Game 1, the Dodgers won the series four games to one.

The Dodgers capped the 2025 season by defeating the Toronto Blue Jays in a dramatic seven-game Series, securing their ninth title. They clinched the Series with a 5–4 extra-innings win in Game 7. Pitcher Yoshinobu Yamamoto delivered an exceptional performance throughout the postseason and earned World Series MVP honors. The victory made the Dodgers the first team in 25 years to repeat as World Series champions. It was the 13th time in a row that they made the playoffs. Only the Atlanta Braves (14) have a longer playoff streak.

For more than a century, Dodgers fans have watched their team build a rich history. That history includes many of MLB's most iconic players who have helped the club win eight World Series titles. Only the Yankees (27), Cardinals (11), and Red Sox (9) have more. The Dodgers feel confident that they will add more championships in coming seasons.

Designated hitter Shohei Ohtani

INDEX